Peddler Arts
Publishing & Design

Color for Clarity
Adult Coloring Book & Meditation Prompts

First Edition

Copyright © 2015 by Kristal Norton
All rights reserved.
ISBN-10: 0692564039
ISBN-13: 978-0692564035

Editor: Becky Cavender
Designer: Kristal Norton
Cover Illustration: Pauline Leger
Artwork: Tara Leaver, Pauline Leger, Kristal Norton,
Alison Russell, Andrea Schroeder, and Rachel Urista

Thank you for buying an authorized edition of this book and for complying with copyright laws by not reproducing, photocopying, scanning, or distributing any part of it in any form without prior written permission of the copyright holder. In doing so, you are supporting the artists and allowing Peddler Arts to continue to publish books.

Printing/manufacturing information for this book may be found on the last page.

A PEDDLER ARTS BOOK

HELLO BEAUTIFUL SOUL,

It is wonderful to be here with you as you enter an inner exploration through coloring.

We all crave moments in our lives where we can ease our minds, take a deep breath, and let go of the stress from our day. During times like this, the inner chatter quiets until a sense of calm comes over us and we can listen to our inner wisdom...the inner wisdom that asks us to be present in a moment and just let go.

But we live in a fast-paced adult world. We work fast. Talk fast. Make quick decisions; reactional decisions. We overwork to the point of exhaustion.

It is possible to reclaim some quiet and calm in our lives. It has been shown that coloring helps us experience that in a simple way.

Repetitive motion, the kind that comes naturally to us – like washing dishes, walking in the woods, or doodling – helps us relax. This is called active meditation.

Active meditation helps me access that place of inner calm much more effectively than sitting in a quiet room with my eyes closed.

And coloring especially lends itself well to this. The sound of a crayon's repetitive strokes on paper brings us to a place of ease. We breathe deeply. Our minds release some tension.

But active meditation through coloring can help us in an even more profound way.

Have you ever experienced a breakthrough to a problem while showering, or doing some other repetitive task? Repetition clears the mind and allows us to work out complex problems subconsciously. We can use coloring as a tool to help us problem solve or become more creative by accessing our inner wisdom.

We all have the answers we seek, right within us.

When I color, I am able relax and reach that place of deep inner knowing. I am able to look within to find the answers.

That's why I designed this coloring book in a way that will help remind you to stay present and listen to your intuition.

Each beautifully designed coloring page, illustrated by six different artists from across the globe, features a word or question to prompt further inner exploration and help you gain clarity in your life.

Flip through the book and intuitively choose a page that calls to you in the moment. Choose colors that speak to you. Don't question or edit yourself. Just trust.

As you color, let your mind wander and explore the word(s) on the page. What thoughts does it bring up for you? What answers lie within?

> You are full of infinite wisdom.
> All you need to do is listen.

With Love,

Kristal

~Kristal Norton
kristalnorton.com
colorforclarity.com

P.S. We would absolutely LOVE to hear your stories about how this book helps you and to see your pages colored in. Share with us by leaving a review on Amazon.com and tag us online with #colorforclarity. We can't wait to hear from you!

PREVIOUS PAGE:

WHAT DO I WANT?
by Pauline Leger

PREVIOUS PAGE:

FOLLOW YOUR DREAMS
by Alison Russell

PREVIOUS PAGE:

TRANSFORM
by Tara Leaver

PREVIOUS PAGE:

FOLLOW YOUR SUNSHINE
by Rachel Urista

PREVIOUS PAGE:
GROW
by Kristal Norton

PREVIOUS PAGE:

YOU ARE MORE THAN YOU THINK YOU ARE
by Andrea Schroeder

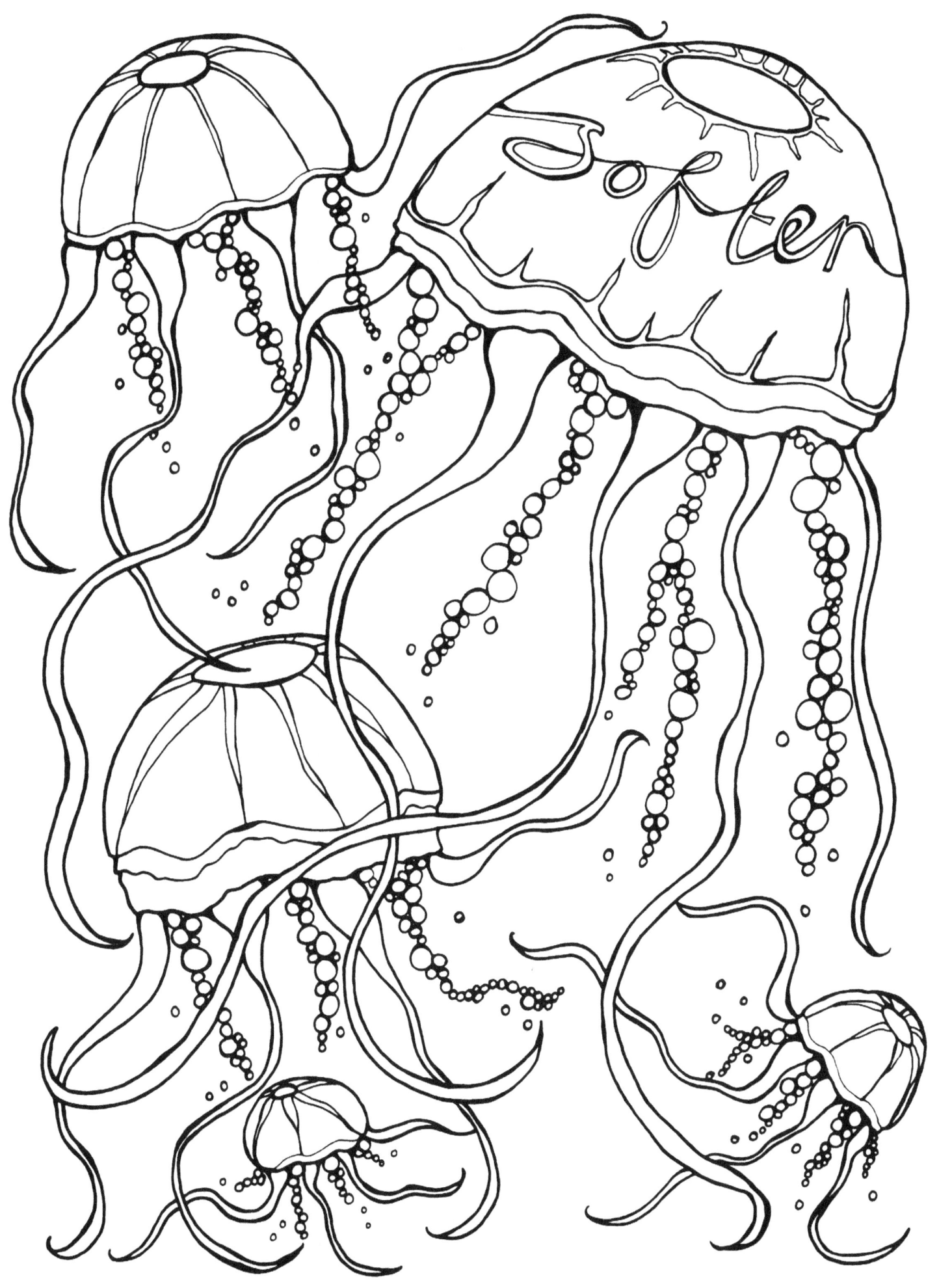

PREVIOUS PAGE:
SOFTEN
by Tara Leaver

PREVIOUS PAGE:

INSPIRE
by Alison Russell

PREVIOUS PAGE:

I AM NOT ALONE
by Pauline Leger

PREVIOUS PAGE:

DRINK IT IN
by Rachel Urista

PREVIOUS PAGE:
IT DOESN'T HAVE TO BE PERFECT
by Tara Leaver

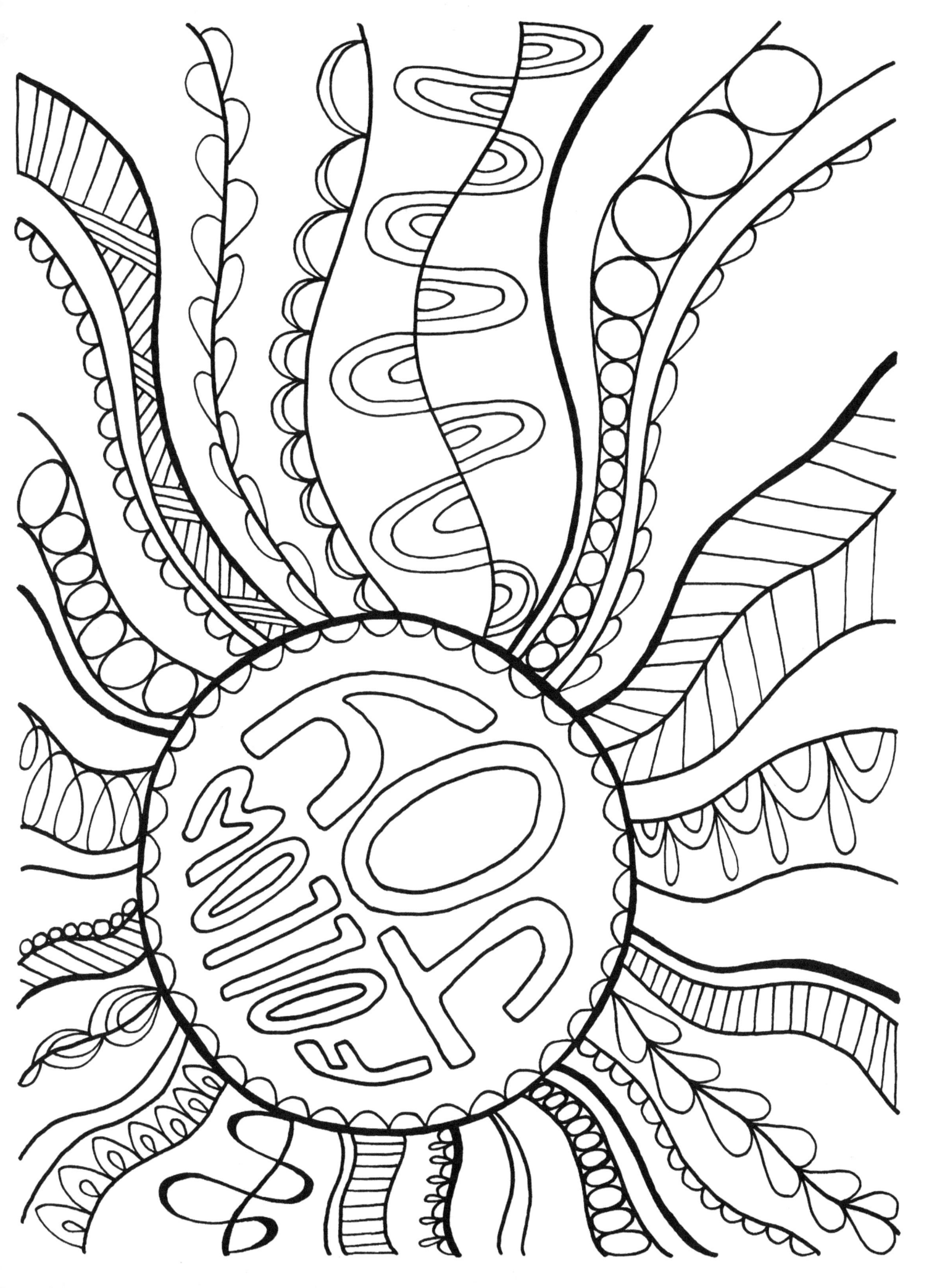

PREVIOUS PAGE:
FOLLOW JOY
by Kristal Norton

PREVIOUS PAGE:

GO WITH THE FLOW
by Alison Russell

PREVIOUS PAGE:

OPEN UP, BUTTERCUP
by Andrea Schroeder

PREVIOUS PAGE:
MAKE SPACE
by Pauline Leger

PREVIOUS PAGE:
REST AND REFLECT
by Rachel Urista

PREVIOUS PAGE:
FIND YOUR WAY
by Tara Leaver

PREVIOUS PAGE:
INNER MAGIC
by Alison Russell

PREVIOUS PAGE:
LOVE OVER FEAR
by Kristal Norton

PREVIOUS PAGE:
JUST BE YOU
by Alison Russell

PREVIOUS PAGE:

EMERGE
by Rachel Urista

PREVIOUS PAGE:
MY VOICE MATTERS
by Pauline Leger

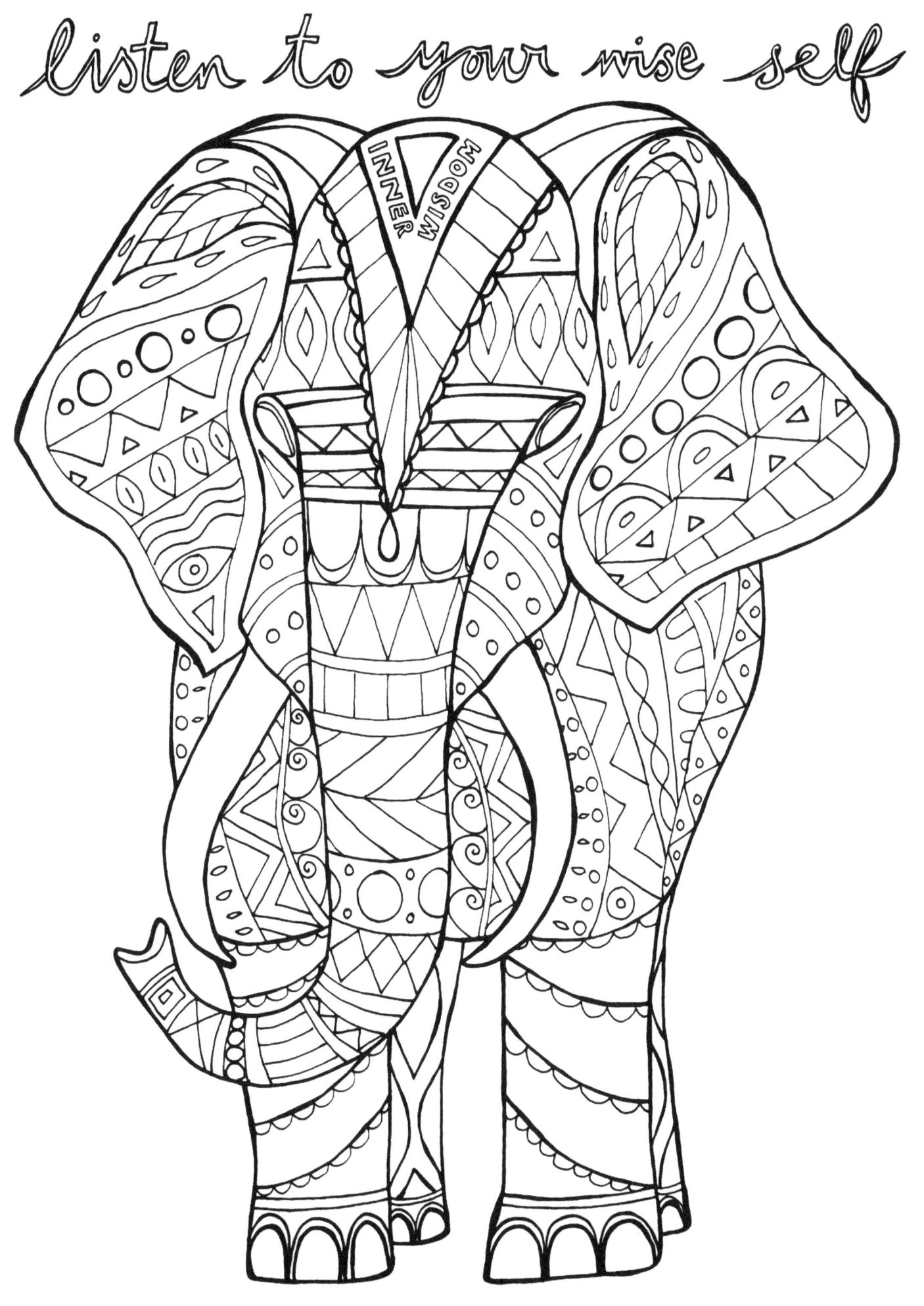

PREVIOUS PAGE:

LISTEN TO YOUR WISE SELF
by Tara Leaver

POTENTIAL EXPANDS

PREVIOUS PAGE:

POTENTIAL EXPANDS
by Andrea Schroeder

PREVIOUS PAGE:
RELAX
by Alison Russell

PREVIOUS PAGE:
REACH FURTHER
by Rachel Urista

PREVIOUS PAGE:

WHAT NEEDS TO BE FORGIVEN?
by Pauline Leger

PREVIOUS PAGE:
JUST BREATHE
by Alison Russell

PREVIOUS PAGE:
WHAT'S NEXT?
by Tara Leaver

PREVIOUS PAGE:
THE HEART KNOWS
by Kristal Norton

PREVIOUS PAGE:
WHAT IF?
by Pauline Leger

PREVIOUS PAGE:

SET SAIL
by Rachel Urista

PREVIOUS PAGE:
MINDFUL
by Alison Russell

PREVIOUS PAGE:

YOU'VE GOT MAGIC IN YOU
by Andrea Schroeder

PREVIOUS PAGE:
FLY
by Pauline Leger

PREVIOUS PAGE:

WHAT DO I NEED?
by Tara Leaver

PREVIOUS PAGE:

OPEN NEW DOORWAYS
by Rachel Urista

PREVIOUS PAGE:
LET IT GO
by Pauline Leger

PREVIOUS PAGE:

PLAY
by Kristal Norton

PREVIOUS PAGE:
RELEASE
by Tara Leaver

PREVIOUS PAGE:

BE A HAPPY CAMPER
by Alison Russell

PREVIOUS PAGE:
LEAP
by Rachel Urista

PREVIOUS PAGE:

TELL YOUR STORY
by Pauline Leger

PREVIOUS PAGE:
FOLLOW YOUR CREATIVE IMPULSE
by Andrea Schroeder

PREVIOUS PAGE:
WHAT ARE MY TINY TREASURES?
by Tara Leaver

PREVIOUS PAGE:

I GLIDE INTO NEW BEGINNINGS
by Rachel Urista

PREVIOUS PAGE:
WE ARE STARDUST
by Pauline Leger

PREVIOUS PAGE:

WANDER THROUGH
by Rachel Urista

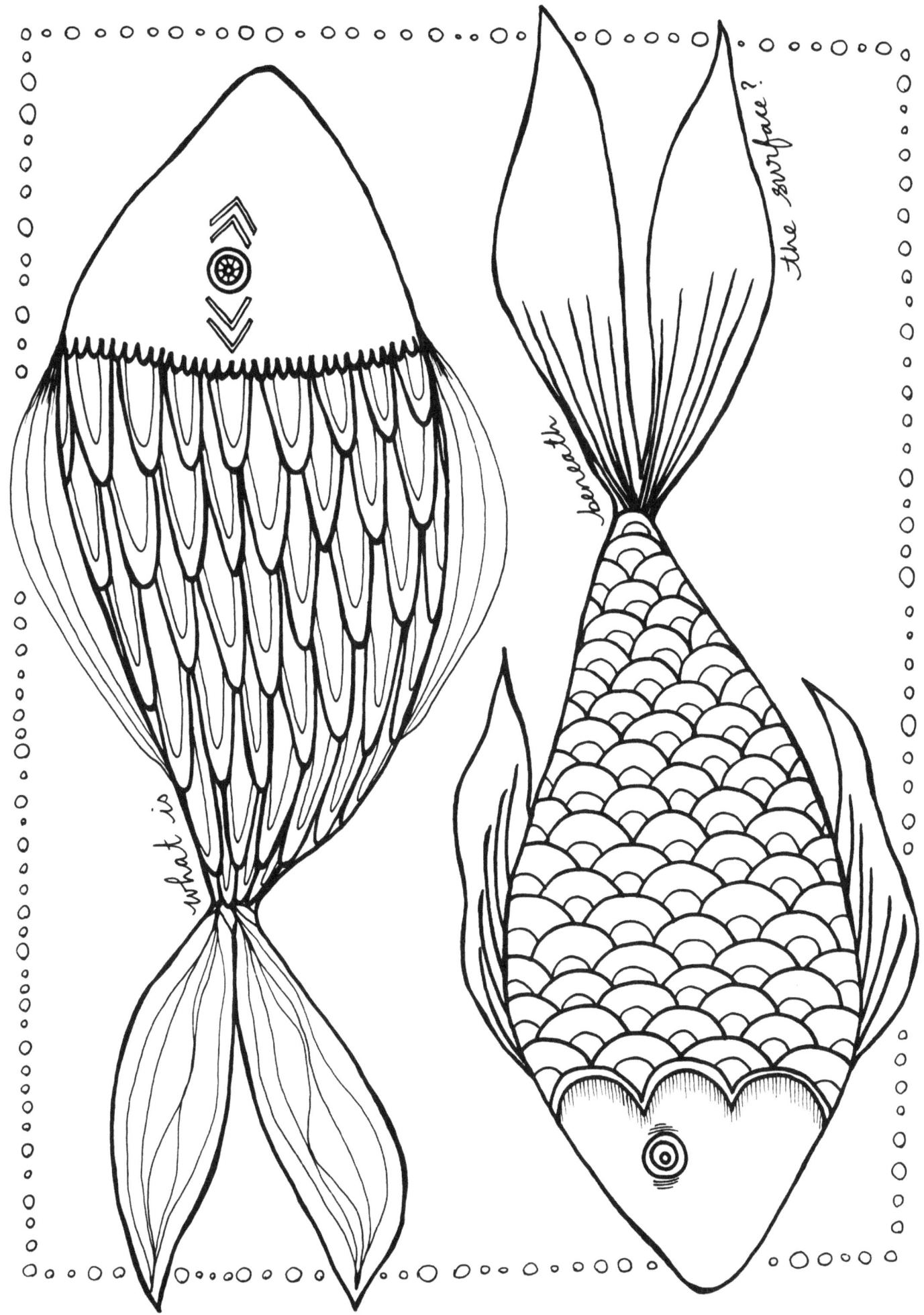

PREVIOUS PAGE:

WHAT IS BENEATH THE SURFACE?
by Tara Leaver

PREVIOUS PAGE:

I AM MEANT TO SHINE
by Kristal Norton

THE ARTISTS

Tara Leaver

Tara is an artist, teacher, writer and creative guide, working from her attic studio by the sea on the south coast of England. She writes about art and creativity on her blog and in her book Creative Spark, and runs online courses which support different aspects of the artistic experience, with a focus on uncovering and developing your natural and unique expression. Her work is mostly about encouraging experimentation with art as self expression and self discovery, and creativity as a lifestyle rather than an item that always ends up somewhere near the bottom of the to do list. Visit Tara at: TaraLeaver.com

Pauline Leger

Pauline is a mixed media artist, writer and graphic designer who believes in the power of inspiration, connection, and in listening to our own hearts. A professional designer for over 25 years, she has designed and illustrated several books and has taught at the Community College. She now focuses her time and energy on teaching the benefits of creativity and on inspiring others to find their own voices through art and journaling. She works from her home in a small coastal community in eastern Canada and is inspired by all that surrounds her. Visit her at: Legerillustrations.blogspot.ca

Kristal Norton

Kristal is a wife, mother, creative explorer, and mixed media artist living by the sea in Connecticut. Her days are led by the belief that taking the time for creative play and to listen to our soul is essential to living a fulfilling life. In her role as a creative life coach, Kristal seeks to help others reclaim and celebrate their innate brilliance through the use of creativity - a hidden power we ALL possess. Learn more about Kristal and her adventures in art journaling and creative soul expression, as she shares her musings on cultivating the authentic self on her website and blog at KristalNorton.com

Alison Russell

Arts and crafts have always been Alison's passion, and over the years she has experimented with many forms such as jewellery making, book binding, and art journaling, to name a few. However, sketching and drawing are what she faithfully returns to. Having grown up in rural Australia, and now living close to the beach with her husband and daughter, Alison finds a lot of inspiration for her art in nature. You can find more of her work at:
www.Facebook.com/PaisleyandBrownPaper

Andrea Schroeder

Andrea is a creative life coach and spiritual teacher living in Winnipeg, Canada. With a paintbrush in one hand & a glitter-gun in the other, she lovingly mentors creative people who want to lead delightfully abundant lives — and do 'impossible' things, with ease & joy. Her mission is to overflow this whole world with sparkly wishes (fulfilled!) and dreams (come true!). Visit Andrea at: CreativeDreamIncubator.com

Photo by Andy Cripe

Rachel Urista

Rachel is a mixed media artist, illustrator and graphic designer living in Oregon. Her lifelong passions for anthropology, mythology, and magic often surface and guide her work. Working from an intuitive place, she journeys through a painting, uncovering the personal myths and messages of each piece along the way. Rachel shows her art at galleries and shares her passion through art journaling and painting workshops. She believes that nourishing your creative self is one of the most loving and powerful things one can do for themselves. Visit Rachel at: RachelUrista.com

www.ingramcontent.com/pod-product-compliance
Lightning Source LLC
Chambersburg PA
CBHW081506040426
42446CB00017B/3422